Klamath Basin
National Wildlife Refuge

Bald eagles can be observed on all
six of the Klamath Basin Refuges...
up to a thousand or more during
the mid-February peak.

It has been said that birds migrating along the Pacific Flyway mirror the pattern of wetlands below. Like stepping stones across a pond–the lakes, rivers, and marshes of the West provide vital resting stops for birds traveling along the flyway. Of all the wetlands in the western United States, no area provides more feeding, resting and nesting habitat than the marshes and lakes of the Klamath Basin. Millions of birds funnel into this wetland oasis to utilize the food and cover of the marshes. This migration to the waters of the Klamath Basin has been enacted for countless generations, evolving long before people arrived to observe this natural wonder.

While much of the Basin's wetlands have been altered or lost in the past one-hundred years, six National Wildlife Refuges and one state wildlife area preserve much of the remaining wildlife habitat. These Refuges remind us of the bounty the Klamath Basin once supported...and to some extent still does.

Utilized by Native people for thousands of years, marsh habitat remains a haven not only for wildlife, but also for humans. Anyone who is thrilled by the call of ten-thousand geese or the image of hundreds of bald eagles in flight will find enrichment here. Whether you come to the Refuges to birdwatch, to hunt, or simply to explore, you will find an experience like no other– because these Refuges have no equal. Those who come to look and listen leave with an understanding that the birds and wildlife of the Klamath Basin express a timeless message to be heeded by all generations.

Opportunities abound for families and children to explore and discover wildlife during all seasons in the Klamath Basin.

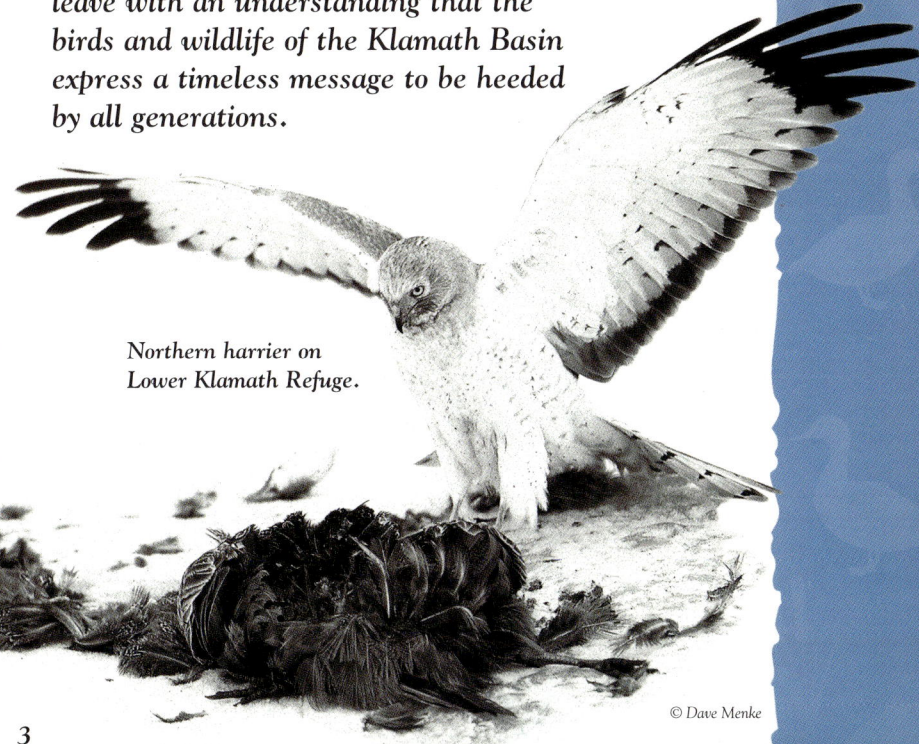

Northern harrier on Lower Klamath Refuge.

© Gary Kramer

Barn owls are present on the Refuges throughout the year.

American coots with their young are a common sight on Lower Klamath, Klamath Marsh and Tule Lake Refuges during the late spring and summer.

© Jeffrey Rich

Evolution is a dance. In this dance, nature leads and each species follows, reacts and adapts. In the Klamath Basin, the dance of evolution has matched millions of resident and migrating birds with a premier wetland oasis. Ever-changing, this unique area and its characteristic wildlife have been dancing together for a very long time.

The headwaters of the Klamath River lie in the northwestern portion of the Basin and Range Province. This area is named for the series of long, narrow north-south mountain ranges which are interspersed with broad basins. One of the distinguishing characteristics of these basins is that most of the water contained within them has no direct outlet to the sea. The Klamath Basin is an exception, however, because the Klamath River cuts through the Cascade Range, channeling water from the Basin to the Pacific Ocean. The Klamath Basin was at one time much wetter than it is today.

During the Pleistocene era, beginning approximately two-million years ago, worldwide temperatures dropped. Continental ice sheets began advancing southward, and rainfall increased. As a result, large rain-fed lakes filled the basins of what is now southern Oregon. The largest of these lakes, known as Lake Modoc, covered over 600,000 acres in the Klamath Basin.

As the ice age ended and temperatures increased, the lakes of the Basin and Range Province slowly began to shrink. By the time John Fremont explored the region in 1844, ancient Lake Modoc had receded to an area of approximately 375,000 acres. This area remained an important oasis for millions of birds, including waterfowl, shorebirds, and marsh birds. These birds used the waters of the Klamath Basin during their migration along the Pacific Flyway and for nesting during the spring.

Huge lakes once covered vast areas of the Klamath Basin. With drier conditions following the last ice age, lakes decreased in size, leaving Klamath Marsh and numerous other shallow wetlands. Mt. Thielsen (shown here) and the Cascade Range form the western boundary of the Klamath Basin.

© Dave Menke

From many points within the Klamath Basin,
14,162-foot Mt. Shasta is prominent on the horizon,
providing a scenic background for both
wildlife viewing and photography.

The riches of the Klamath Basin were utilized by Native peoples for thousands of years. Rather than adapting the surroundings to fit their needs, early inhabitants adapted themselves to fit the rhythm of the natural environment. In this manner, the original Klamath people were an integral part of the marsh ecosystem.

It is uncertain when people first arrived in the Klamath Basin. The Modoc and Klamath Indians (who may be descendants of the first inhabitants) have no stories describing their arrival. Instead, their oral history describes their creation as a people concurrent with the creation of the marshes of the Klamath Basin. Archeological evidence supports the theory that people have occupied the Klamath Basin continuously for as long as 11,000 years.

The Modoc and Klamath people lived in tune with the seasons of the marsh and the surrounding Great Basin desert. In the spring, stores of protein were obtained from the harvest of fish. These fish, mainly suckers and salmon, were dried on racks and later stored in underground pits. Also at this time of year, bird eggs were gathered from nests hidden among the marsh grasses. During the summer, women gathered many plants, including camas and ipo bulbs. In the northern portion of the Basin it was more common to gather yellow water lily seeds.

This plant, called wocus, was prepared in a variety of ways, and provided a much-needed supply of starch in the Indian diet. Game animals such as deer and elk were available all year. At higher elevations, men used bow and arrows to kill antelope and big-horned sheep. Both black and grizzly bears were killed for their fur. A variety of smaller animals, including gray wolves, foxes, badgers, wildcats and coyotes were also used for food and clothing. In late summer, berries, fruits, and seeds became available. People moved to the locales where these foods were ripening. During the summer and fall migrations, a variety of birds were eaten including coots, ducks, geese, swans, pelicans, grebes, herons, cormorants, plovers, and gulls.

With the coming of the first snows, the people of the marsh assembled their winter homes and prepared for a long, dormant season. With wood gathered, food stored, and furs prepared, the winter months were mostly spent in shelters. Long winter hours were spent weaving, dancing, and visiting friends and family. By the time the first geese appeared over the marshes in spring, the Klamath people would once again prepare for the return of the sucker fish. This completed another cycle in the lives of a people who moved with the rhythms of the marshes that surrounded them.

Coyotes are the most commonly observed predatory mammal in the Klamath Basin.

Yellow water lily, known as wocus, *was an important food used by Klamath Indians. Dugout canoes were used to harvest the pods of this marsh plant. The seeds were later converted to foodstuffs in several steps involving fermenting, drying, ageing and cooking.*

© Jeffrey Rich

Black-necked stilts commonly nest at the water's edge in shallow wetlands.

Unlike the Native peoples of the Klamath Region, the white settlers who filtered into the Basin did not intend to live wholly off the natural bounty of the marshes and wetlands. Instead, they brought with them a modern ideology equating the value of land with the financial prosperity it could produce. As they converted this ideology into action, the new inhabitants began to have a profound and lasting effect on the Native people and wildlife of the Klamath Basin.

The first non-natives arrived in the Klamath Basin in the 1840's searching for beaver. The area did not contain enough beaver to attract many trappers. However, settlers who came later along the Applegate Trail *did* find the area suitable for ranching and farming. By the 1870's, a few hundred emigrants had settled in the area. They pastured livestock on native grasses and on cultivated rye grass.

As a result of a treaty in the early 1860's, the people of the Klamath and Modoc tribes had been moved to a single Indian reservation near Upper Klamath Lake. Some Modocs were unhappy sharing land with the Klamaths. They wished to return to their homeland near Tule and Lower Klamath Lakes. In 1872-73, a series of skirmishes and battles took place in and around the present day Lava Beds National Monument. The Modocs held out against a large U.S. Army force until their need for food and water finally forced them to surrender.

The defeat of the Modocs signified the end of their ancient way of life in the Klamath Basin. No longer would these people be dependent on the natural cycles of the marshes and uplands for their food and livelihood. The new inhabitants brought their own sources of food in the form of seeds and livestock. With the opportunity for irrigation and trade, the desire to maintain healthy wetlands diminished in importance. The resulting changes to the Basin's ecology were swift and dramatic.

© Dave Menke

Raccoons occur on all of the Klamath Basin Refuges.

© Dave Menke

Mule deer are abundant and easily seen all year on the six units of the Klamath Basin Refuges.

Facing east from Sheepy Ridge, a person can look down upon the flat basin floor and see farmlands extending as far as the eye can see. One can imagine all this farmland covered by shallow lakes and marshes. Perhaps the men who designed the Klamath Reclamation Project hiked up this ridge, looked down upon the vast expanse of Tule Lake, and envisioned hundreds of small farms covering this broad, flat basin. It has been said if you can envision something in a dream, you can achieve it. This was certainly true for the people who came to the Klamath Basin dreaming of what was one of the first large reclamation projects in the United States.

The potential of wide scale drainage in the Klamath Basin for agricultural production on irrigated farms was soon realized. Following the Reclamation Act of 1902, and the ceding of land by Oregon and California to the federal government, work began on the Klamath Reclamation Project. The goal of this federally legislated project was to convert thousands of acres of marshland into small family farms. The use of irrigation greatly increased crop yields. In 1906, the newly formed Reclamation Service was given authorization to lower the water level of Upper Klamath Lake and to reclaim Lower Klamath, Tule, Clear, Goose Lakes, "...and any river or body of water connected therewith."

By the time work was completed, wetlands in and around the Klamath Basin had been reduced to just twenty-five percent of their original size. These former wetlands were converted to about 240,000 acres of irrigated farmlands.

As reclamation work progressed, the birds of Lower Klamath and Tule Lakes were threatened by both habitat loss and market hunters. Because of its unique ecology, Lower Klamath Lake contained numerous islands of emergent vegetation interspersed with channels of open water. This habitat supported many colonies of nesting birds, such as western grebes, cormorants, white pelicans, gulls, and terns. Because of their communal nesting habits, thousands of these birds were easily killed. So many of these birds were eliminated from the area around Lower Klamath Lake that a nationwide movement was initiated to prevent their eradication. Ducks, who also used Lower Klamath and Tule Lakes for breeding, were extensively hunted for their meat. Much of this was shipped to San Francisco markets. Birds were taken in such numbers from Lower Klamath and Tule Lakes that professional hunters, themselves, called for a moratorium on shooting during the breeding season. This was rejected by local residents who felt a moratorium would impinge on their freedom to hunt. Eventually, federal protection was obtained for all migrating birds.

Sandhill cranes nest in meadows and grasslands on Lower Klamath and Klamath Marsh Refuges.

American avocets are one of the many species dependent on shallow marshes for feeding and nesting habitat.

Western grebe "bathing" on Lower Klamath Refuge.

© Jeffrey Rich

Shallow marshes in the Klamath Basin provide ideal nesting and brood rearing habitat for cinnamon teal and many other duck species.

© Dave Menke

Refuges

There is a tendency in nature to maintain a sense of balance, and the same can be said of human nature. By the early part of the century, the natural system in the Klamath Basin had been vastly altered and it became clear that a more balanced approach was needed. Citizens concerned about the welfare of the birds were instrumental in the creation of the Klamath Basin National Wildlife Refuges.

Lower Klamath was the first of six National Wildlife Refuges to be established in the Klamath Basin. It was the first of many wildlife refuges throughout the nation to be set aside to protect migratory waterfowl. The impetus to establish Lower Klamath as a Refuge came from members of the National Audubon Society, among others, who were witnessing the rapid decimation of many bird species. Originally named the Klamath Lake Reservation, this 81,619 acre area of lakes and marshes was reserved on August 8, 1908 by President Theodore Roosevelt "for the use of the Department of Agriculture as a preserve and breeding grounds for native birds."

Although marsh bird numbers rebounded after the establishment of the Lower Klamath Reservation, this abundance was not to last. Because the Refuge was superimposed on lands which had been ceded to the United States for reclamation, it was subject to other demands such as farming and flood control. Just nine years after the Refuge was established, its main source of water, a channel of the Klamath River, was blocked by railroad construction. By 1921, Lower Klamath Lake, which had once supported 3,500 white pelican nests, 400 cormorant nests, 600 great blue heron nests, 1,200 western grebe nests, and untold thousands of waterfowl, had been reduced to a huge, dry, alkaline dustbowl.

White pelicans nest in isolated locations on Lower Klamath, Clear Lake, and Upper Klamath Refuges.

© Larry Turner

12

In the late nineteenth and early twentieth century, commercial hunters killed waterfowl by the thousands on Tule Lake Refuge. Today the Tule Lake Marsh is a popular sport hunting mecca for waterfowl hunters. Sport hunting is carefully regulated to insure the continuation of healthy populations of all species.

Prior to its establishment as a Refuge in 1928, the area in and around Tule Lake had lost much of its marsh habitat. Irrigation diversion had reduced both the size and the depth of the lake. With dwindling marshes and water, the birds of the Tule Lake area were easy targets for hunters. This situation prompted concern for the region's wildlife. In 1928, President Coolidge established Tule Lake as a "refuge and breeding ground for birds." From its inception, the Refuge has been managed jointly by the Fish and Wildlife Service, and the Bureau of Reclamation.

A water issue eventually led the Bureau of Reclamation to revive Lower Klamath Lake as a wetland. Tule Lake's reduced size was inadequate to prevent periodic flooding of the surrounding farmlands. To alleviate this problem, a plan was formulated to drill a tunnel through Sheepy Ridge to the dry Lower Klamath lakebed. The first water was released through the tunnel from Tule Lake in 1942. While this solution helped revive the marshes of Lower Klamath Refuge, it still left the Refuges dependent on the Klamath Irrigation Project for water to maintain marshes. Due to competing demands, the water eventually reaching the lower Refuges is sometimes inadequate, particularly in times of drought. Unaware of the politics of water allocation, migrating waterfowl come to the Refuges each fall

expecting the marshes to provide food and shelter. The millions of birds dependent upon these wetlands make it vitally important that Lower Klamath, Tule Lake and Upper Klamath Refuges receive adequate water supplies.

In addition to Lower Klamath and Tule Lake, there are four other Refuges in the Klamath Basin National Wildlife Refuge complex. Clear Lake Refuge lies southeast of Tule Lake and serves as both a source of irrigation water and an important nesting area for white pelicans and other colonial nesting species. In addition to the lake, this Refuge contains over 9,000 acres of surrounding uplands providing habitat for pronghorn antelope, mule deer, and sage grouse.

© Dave Menke

Sage grouse inhabit the uplands around Clear Lake Refuge.

River otter on Lower Klamath Refuge.

© Dave Menke

© Howard West

Mountain bluebirds nest along the forested edges of Klamath Marsh.

Pronghorn antelope forage in both farmlands and grasslands in the southern Klamath Basin, and can be seen throughout the year.

© Dave Menke

Accessible mainly by boat, Upper Klamath Refuge is located in the northwest corner of Upper Klamath Lake. This habitat consists almost entirely of marsh and open water. Established in 1928, Upper Klamath Refuge provides important nesting habitat for waterfowl and colonial nesting birds such as pelicans, egrets, and herons.

Klamath Marsh Refuge, located 50 miles north of Klamath Falls, is made up of low-lying marshland dominated by bulrush and sedges. This area supports large numbers of both migrating and nesting waterfowl. The surrounding meadows attract sandhill cranes, numerous shorebirds, and several species of raptors. Up to 150 Rocky Mountain elk use the Refuge during the late summer and fall.

Bear Valley was the last Refuge to be established in the Klamath Basin. It is located thirteen miles southwest of Klamath Falls in a forest of mature pine, fir and cedar trees. Bear Valley Refuge was established to protect roosting bald eagles from November to March. Bald eagles return to the Basin each winter attracted by large concentrations of waterfowl. Established in 1978, Bear Valley Refuge protects night roosting habitat for several hundred bald eagles and has become an important area for the study, observation, and preservation of our national symbol.

During the winter, after most migrants have flown south, bald eagles compete with one another to feed on the remaining waterfowl on Tule Lake and Lower Klamath Refuges.

© Robert C. Fields

Native peoples, who first came to the Basin over ten-thousand years ago, had little impact on the migratory birds and wildlife populations of the region. With the coming of Europeans, however, the degree of impact grew to the point of endangering some native species. Fortunately, this trend was recognized in time to save much of the area's wildlife. The role the Refuges have played in this effort has evolved over time. After years of working to bring back the dwindling numbers of birds, refuge managers now realize that the only way to ensure healthy wildlife populations is by enhancing or mimicking the natural cycles inherent in each habitat. The benefits of this approach to management can be seen in the enormous variety of wildlife which still inhabit the marshes and uplands of the Klamath Basin Refuges today.

Many different management techniques are used on the Refuges, all of which focus on the main goal of preserving and enhancing the habitats on which wildlife depend. Refuge managers use farming, grazing, burning, flooding and other techniques to increase the diversity and productivity of habitats. On the permanently flooded marshes of Lower Klamath Lake, emergent plants such as bulrush and cattail predominate. These islands of vegetation provide important nesting sites, food, and cover for a variety of birds. In addition, marshes allow submergent plants such as sago pondweed and coontail to proliferate. These underwater plants are both food for waterfowl and a growth medium for invertebrates eaten by many birds and fish.

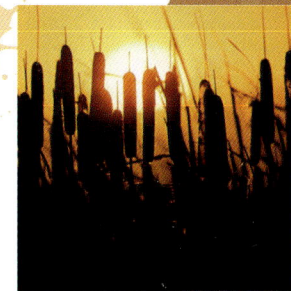

© Gary R. Zahn

Cattails surrounding marshes provide habitat for marsh wrens, yellow-headed blackbirds and other species.

Placing leg bands on ducks helps biologists track their seasonal movements and determine information such as longevity and productivity.

© Don Jackson

Migrating waterfowl benefit from the waste grain left after crops are harvested on the Refuges and other locations in the Klamath Basin.

© Richard Voss

Burning overgrown marshes is one method managers use to restore productive wetlands on the Refuges.

In contrast to permanent marshes, seasonally flooded marshes are managed to encourage a different variety of plants. Following the natural water cycle of the West, seasonal marshes dry out during the summer and plants such as red goosefoot and smartweed take hold. These plants provide important food and cover for fall migrating waterfowl. In the past, fires started either by Native people or by lightning, helped control the overgrowth of brush and trees. Today's managers use prescribed burns to remove brush thus allowing grasses and broad-leafed plants to become established. These plants provide protected sites and food for many nesting birds as well as cover for pronghorn antelope and mule deer.

By studying the natural processes at work in the Basin, refuge managers have been able to maintain healthy populations of most native species. From the forests of the Klamath Marsh, to the dry uplands surrounding Clear Lake, to the waters of Upper Klamath Refuge, each area is managed to maximize the natural diversity of habitats which is nature's trademark.

Yellow-bellied marmot on Lower Klamath Refuge.

Prior to the mid 1980's white-faced ibis were only rarely seen in the Klamath Basin. In recent years up to 2,000 or more pairs have set up nesting colonies primarily in the hardstem bulrush marshes of Lower Klamath Refuge. Biologists think these birds moved into the Basin when marshes surrounding the Great Salt Lake and on Malheur National Wildlife Refuge flooded nesting sites, thus forcing the ibis to search for suitable nesting habitat elsewhere.

Northern shovelers are seen in large
flocks on Lower Klamath Refuge in
the late fall and winter.

Life at the Klamath Basin Refuges is never quiet. Whether you visit during the summer, winter, spring, or fall a unique interplay of wildlife can be observed. Many of the 263 species of birds using the Refuges are migrants; they come and go at varying times. Their passage marks the seasons on the Refuges in an endless cycle of arrivals and departures. In addition, many species of birds and mammals remain in the Basin throughout the year. From mating, to rearing young, to gathering food, these wild residents are an integral part of the continuous cycle of life which can be observed and enjoyed throughout the year on the Klamath Basin Refuges.

Because the Klamath Basin is visited by three-quarters of the waterfowl migrating along the Pacific Flyway, fall is a very dynamic time. By late October, as migrating waterfowl reach peak numbers, one-to two-million ducks and geese are seen on the Refuges. By December, as the weather begins to turn cold and marshes freeze, many waterfowl move south. Those that remain, attract thousands of raptors, including bald eagles, northern harriers, and red-tailed and rough-legged hawks. The eagles, which have migrated from Alaska, British Columbia, Washington, and Oregon, can be seen feeding on the icy marshes of the lower Refuges until late

February. These eagles roost in large concentrations in Bear Valley Refuge and can be observed flying out of this canyon *en mass* during the chilly pre-dawn hours.

By early spring, all but a handful of the bald eagles have begun their northward migration. About this time, shorebirds and waterfowl begin filtering back onto the Refuges from the south. Many of these birds will remain in the Klamath Basin to nest. Thousands of ducks, geese, and shorebirds are raised on the Refuges each year. Clear Lake Refuge, for example, is colonized each spring by white pelicans. These gregarious birds nest safely on the lake's islands which cannot be reached by terrestrial predators. In addition to all of the waterfowl and shorebirds, the Klamath Refuges provide important nesting habitat for a variety of songbirds. Warblers, sparrows, and blackbirds are just a few of the many songbirds which can be seen and heard on the refuges.

During the spring and summer, the results of the hard work of building nests can be seen as young broods of ducks and geese follow behind their parents. Later in the summer the adult waterfowl, which have molted and are flightless, utilize the safety of the marsh vegetation for cover and food. By the time the adults have reared their broods and regained their flight feathers, the first of the fall migrants arrive, thus marking the start of yet another cycle of activity on the Klamath Basin Refuges.

© Dean Baker

© Howard West

Although primarily nocturnal, bobcats are sometimes seen during the day along Sheepy Ridge separating Tule Lake and Lower Klamath Refuges.

In addition to waterfowl, marsh birds such as this black-crowned night-heron benefit from the wetland habitats on the Refuges.

© Howard West

© Jeffrey Rich

A ruddy duck "shows off" in spring courtship display.

The story of human occupation of the Klamath Basin is really the story of our struggle to find our place in the natural world. In this arena, we are trying to find ways to use the natural resources of the Basin without destroying its very fabric. At the same time, people are seeking ways to enhance their own lives while protecting the Basin's unique wildlife heritage. We do not yet have all the answers to these very difficult challenges. Fortunately, nature has been a patient partner, ever ready to respond to our attempts at peacemaking.

Maintaining a stable water supply to support refuge wetlands poses the biggest challenge to the Klamath Basin Refuges and its wildlife. With a limited and sometimes unpredictable supply, both water quality and availability are major refuge concerns. A similar scenario has been playing out all over the West resulting in a drastic reduction in the wetlands available to waterfowl in the Pacific Flyway. This lack of wetland habitat has resulted in higher bird concentrations believed to contribute to waterfowl diseases such as avian botulism and fowl cholera.

Along with the issues of water and land use, the overall status of our National Wildlife Refuge System is continually being scrutinized. Attempts to change the focus of Refuges to include human uses such as mining, oil development, motorized recreation, and commercial enterprise, could jeopardize much of the wildlife habitat the Refuges have been established to protect.

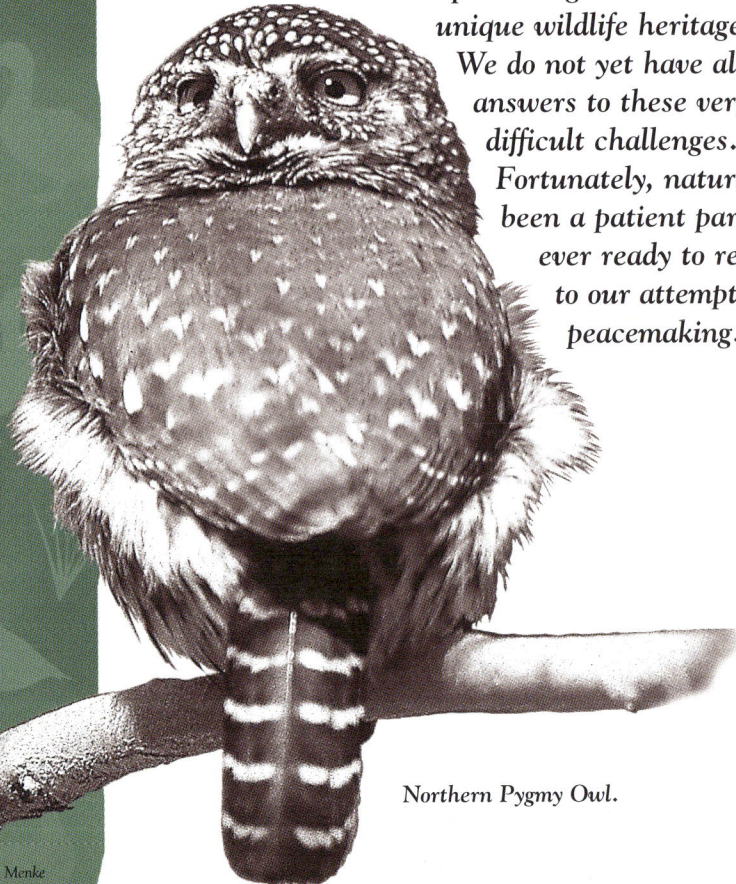
Northern Pygmy Owl.

© Dave Menke

California gull nestlings begin life on a small island in Lower Klamath National Wildlife Refuge.

© E. J. O'Neill

Unfortunately, there are no guarantees that the majesty of the Klamath Basin National Wildlife Refuges will be able to coexist with modern society.

There are many ways individuals can help maintain and restore the wildlife of the Klamath Basin and other wild places. An appreciation of the diversity and complexity of the natural environment helps us understand the issues. The Refuges belong to all of us and their fate is in all of our hands. Volunteering, contributing financially, and writing to Congress about the need for legislative support for our National Wildlife Refuge System are all important ways of showing you care. Perhaps the best way to help ensure the future of the Klamath Basin Refuges, however, is to visit, enjoy, and tell others about them. Every visitor to the Refuges gains a unique impression of their majesty: from the canoeist awestruck by the enormous beaver lodges on the Upper Klamath Refuge, to the birder adding a new species of shorebird for her life list, to the child watching a coyote for the first time, the wonders and secrets of the Klamath Basin are limitless. By visiting the Klamath Refuges you will come to own a little part of them. It is this ownership which leads to concern, and with enough concern, protection is ensured.

Tiny but ferocious, a long-tailed weasel will sometimes attack prey several times its size and weight.

© Howard West

Mule deer winter along the boundary of Lave Beds National Monument at the south edge of Tule Lake National Wildlife Refuge.

© Jeffrey Rich

© Howard West

Seasonal Wildlife Happenings and Refuge Events

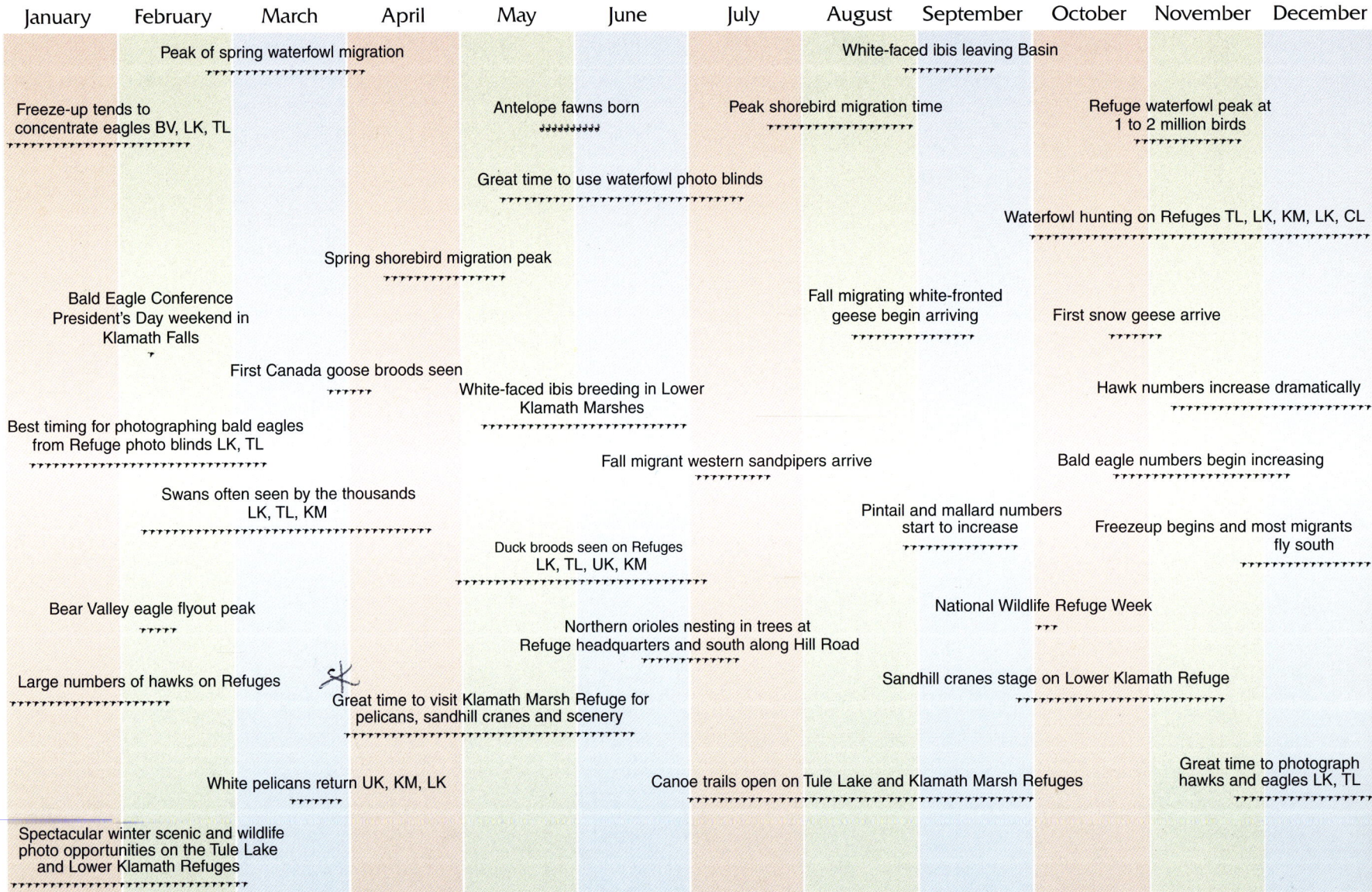

January	February	March	April	May	June	July	August	September	October	November	December

Peak of spring waterfowl migration

White-faced ibis leaving Basin

Freeze-up tends to concentrate eagles BV, LK, TL

Antelope fawns born

Peak shorebird migration time

Refuge waterfowl peak at 1 to 2 million birds

Great time to use waterfowl photo blinds

Waterfowl hunting on Refuges TL, LK, KM, LK, CL

Spring shorebird migration peak

Bald Eagle Conference President's Day weekend in Klamath Falls

Fall migrating white-fronted geese begin arriving

First snow geese arrive

First Canada goose broods seen

White-faced ibis breeding in Lower Klamath Marshes

Hawk numbers increase dramatically

Best timing for photographing bald eagles from Refuge photo blinds LK, TL

Fall migrant western sandpipers arrive

Bald eagle numbers begin increasing

Swans often seen by the thousands LK, TL, KM

Pintail and mallard numbers start to increase

Freezeup begins and most migrants fly south

Duck broods seen on Refuges LK, TL, UK, KM

Bear Valley eagle flyout peak

Northern orioles nesting in trees at Refuge headquarters and south along Hill Road

National Wildlife Refuge Week

Large numbers of hawks on Refuges

Sandhill cranes stage on Lower Klamath Refuge

Great time to visit Klamath Marsh Refuge for pelicans, sandhill cranes and scenery

White pelicans return UK, KM, LK

Canoe trails open on Tule Lake and Klamath Marsh Refuges

Great time to photograph hawks and eagles LK, TL

Spectacular winter scenic and wildlife photo opportunities on the Tule Lake and Lower Klamath Refuges

Refuges Key: LK=Lower Klamath; TL=Tule Lake; KM=Klamath Marsh; UK=Upper Klamath; CL=Clear Lake; BV=Bear Valley

When to Visit

With over 400 species of wildlife found on the Klamath Basin Refuges, there is always something interesting to see. The nearly constant arrivals and departures of wildlife, along with the changing seasons and weather, make the Klamath Basin a very dynamic place to observe wildlife. Notable highlights include the peak waterfowl migration periods during mid-November and again in early April and the gathering of over 1,000 bald eagles on the Refuges in mid-February. Other opportunities are limitless. While canoeing on Upper Klamath Refuge you may come across a family of river otters at play...or you may see an osprey carrying fish after fish to the young in its nest. These are just a few of the rewards you may receive when you visit the Klamath Basin Refuges.

Pintail and Mallard ducks nest near refuge wetlands with numbers of both into the hundreds-of-thousands during the fall and spring migrations.

Upper Klamath National Wildlife Refuge

Recreation Creek
Malone Springs Boat Launch
Crystal Creek
Rock Point Boat Launch
FOREST NATIONAL Road
WINEMA NATIONAL
West Side
AGENCY LAKE
UPPER KLAMATH LAKE
140

LEGEND
Refuge Boundary
Marsh
Canoe Trail

0 1 2 Miles
0 1.6 3.2 Kilometers

KLAMATH MARSH REFUGE

CRATER LAKE
NATIONAL PARK
Sand Creek
97
62
Fort Klamath
Chiloquin
UPPER KLAMATH REFUGE
140
UPPER KLAMATH LAKE
HANKS MARSH
UPPER KLAMATH REFUGE
97

KLAMATH BASIN
National Wildlife Refuges

OREGON
CALIFORNIA
Area Enlarged

Klamath Marsh National Wildlife Refuge

Refuge Headquarters
Military Crossing
Big Springs Creek
Williamson River
Silver Lake Road
Williamson River
97
Little Wocus Bay
KLAMATH MARSH
Wocus Bay

LEGEND
Refuge Boundary
Canoe Area (July 1 - Sept. 30)
Marsh
Recreation Trail

0 1 2 Miles
0 1.6 3.2 Kilometers

Spencer Creek
KLAMATH WILDLIFE AREA (State of Oregon)
Klamath Falls
140
140
70 Bonanza
39
N

0 5 10 Miles
0 8 16 Kilometers

66
BEAR VALLEY REFUGE
Worden
OREGON CALIFORNIA
Lost River
Merrill
161
139 Tulelake
TULE LAKE REFUGE
OREGON CALIFORNIA
Lost River
Clear Lake Reservoir
Willow Creek

Dorris
LOWER KLAMATH REFUGE
Refuge Headquarters and Visitor Center
LAVA BEDS NATIONAL MONUMENT
97
CLEAR LAKE REFUGE

Bear Valley National Wildlife Refuge

To Keno
Keno Worden Road
BEAR VALLEY
Pearson Butte
WORDEN
Southern Pacific
97

LEGEND
Refuge Boundary
Observation Area

0 1 Miles
0 1.6 Kilometers
N

Clear Lake National Wildlife Refuge

Lost River
Willow Creek
CLEAR LAKE RESERVOIR
Peninsula
Clear Lake Reservoir
Willow Creek
N
MODOC   NATIONAL   FOREST
Forest Service Road 136
To Hwy 139

LEGEND
Marsh
Refuge Boundary
Unpaved Road

0 1 2 Miles
0 1.6 3.2 Kilometers

30

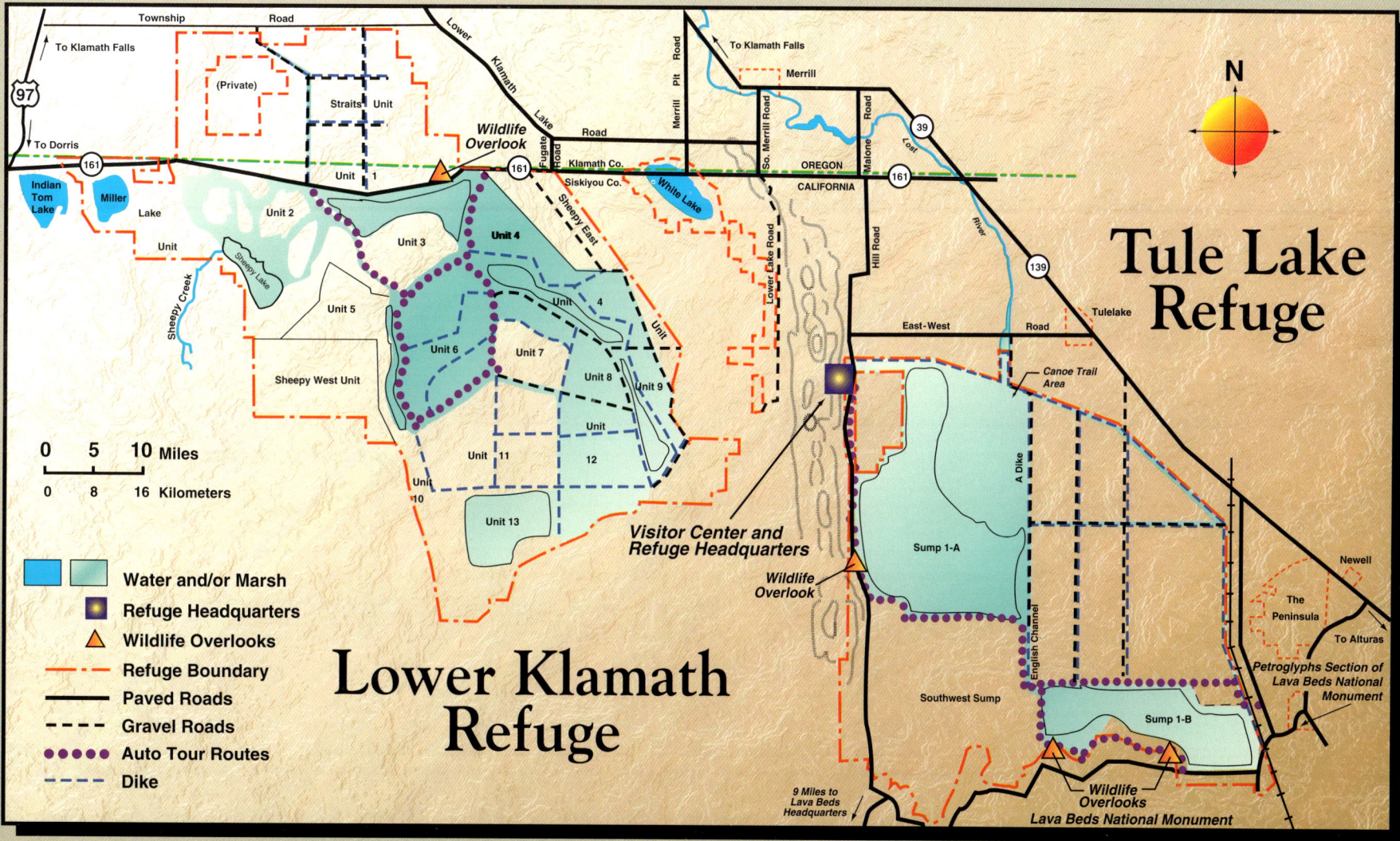

N

To Klamath Falls

Township Road

To Klamath Falls

(Private)

Straits Unit

Merrill

Lower Klamath Lake Road

OREGON
CALIFORNIA

Wildlife Overlook

Unit 1

Klamath Co.
Siskiyou Co.

Merrill Pit Road

So. Merrill Road

Malone Road

*Tule Lake
Refuge*

Indian Tom Lake

Miller Lake

Unit

Lake

Unit 2

Sheepy Creek

Sheepy Lake

Unit 3

Unit 4

Sheepy East

White Lake

Lower Lake Road

Hill Road

Lost River

Tulelake

Unit 5

Unit 4

Unit 6

Unit 7

Unit 8

Unit

Unit 9

Canoe Trail Area

East-West Road

Sheepy West Unit

A Dike

0 5 10 Miles
0 8 16 Kilometers

Unit 11

Unit

12

Unit

Sump 1-A

Newell

Visitor Center and
Refuge Headquarters

Unit
10

Unit 13

Wildlife Overlook

English Channel

The Peninsula

To Alturas

Petroglyphs Section of
Lava Beds National
Monument

Southwest Sump

Sump 1-B

Water and/or Marsh

Refuge Headquarters

Wildlife Overlooks

Refuge Boundary

Paved Roads

Gravel Roads

Auto Tour Routes

Dike

*Lower Klamath
Refuge*

9 Miles to
Lava Beds
Headquarters

Wildlife Overlooks
Lava Beds National Monument

Lower Klamath and Tule Lake National Wildlife Refuges

Acknowledgements

This booklet was researched and written by Kari Tuck. We are grateful for review and editorial comments provided by Laura Allen, Betty Lou Byrne-Shirley, Akimi King, Pat McMillan, Dave Mauser, Dave Menke, Marshall Staunton, Tom Stewart, and Wendell Wood.

Contributing photographers are Dean Baker, Robert C. Fields, Don Jackson, Gary Kramer, Dave Menke, E. J. O'Neill, Jeffrey Rich, Larry Turner, Richard Voss, Howard West and Gary R. Zahm.

Design by Mary Hyde Martin Design and printing by Ram Offset Lithographers.

Financial support provided by the San Francisco Bay Wildlife Society and the Klamath Basin Wildlife Association.

Front Cover: Mt. Shasta forms a backdrop for many wildlife observations on the Klamath Basin Refuges as in this scene of cackling Canada geese on Tule Lake Refuge during the fall migration. © Robert C. Fields

Back Cover: Dense concentrations of snow and Ross' geese are seen feeding on Tule Lake Refuge as numbers peak in early to mid-November. © Jeffrey Rich

Published by:

The Klamath Basin Wildlife Association
Rt. 1, Box 74
Tulelake, CA 96134
(916) 667-2231
530

ISBN 0-9649328-1-4